ENRICO IV

*Luigi Pirandello
adapted by
Richard Nelson*

BROADWAY PLAY PUBLISHING INC
New York
www.broadwayplaypublishing.com
info@broadwayplaypublishing.com

ENRICO IV

© Copyright 2001 Richard Nelson

Cover photo by Kevin Berne

First published by B P P I in an Acting Edition: October 2001

This edition: October 2017

I S B N: 978-0-88145-739-1

Assistant to the Publisher (2001): Michele Travis
Book design: Marie Donovan
Word processing: Microsoft Word for Windows
Typographic controls: Xerox Ventura Publisher 2.0 P E
Typeface: Palatino
Copy editing (2001): Sue Gilad

ENRICO IV was commissioned, developed and produced by American Conservatory Theater (Carey Perloff, Artistic Director; Heather Kitchen, Managing Director) in San Francisco CA, opening 4 April 2001, at the Geary Theater. The cast and creative contributors were:

ENRICO IV	Marco Barricelli
DONNA MATILDA	Felicity Jones
FRIDA	Claire Winters
CHARLES DI NOLLI	David Mendelsohn
TITO BELCREDI	Anthony Fusco
DOCTOR DIONYSUS GENONI	Charles Lanyer
HAROLD	Douglas Nolan
ORDULPH	Benton Greene
LANDOLPH	Tommy A Gomez
BERTHOLD	Chris Ferry
JOHN	Tom Blair
YOUNG SERVANTS	Scott Asti, Samuel R Gates

Director	Carey Perloff
Set design	Ralph Funicello
Lighting design	Peter Maradudin
Costume design	Deborah Dryden
Sound design	Garth Hemphill
Original music	David Lang
Dramaturg	Paul Walsh
Fight director	Gregory Hoffman
Hair and makeup	Rick Echols
Stage manager	Kimberly Mark Webb

CHARACTERS & SETTING

"ENRICO IV"
DONNA MATILDA
FRIDA, *her daughter*
CHARLES DI NOLLI, *engaged to* FRIDA
TITO BELCREDI, DONNA MATILDA'*s lover*
DOCTOR DIONYSUS GENONI
HAROLD
ORDULPH
LANDOLPH
BERTHOLD
JOHN, *an old servant*
two YOUNG SERVANTS

This translation is based up an English version by
Edward Storer (1922).

ACT ONE

*(The "throne room" of the villa, decorated to be an exact
replica of* ENRICO IV's *throne room at Goslar. Two large
paintings, one of a man dressed as* ENRICO *and the other of
a woman dressed as the marchioness* MATILDA *of Tuscany.
Two young servants, dressed in eleventh-century costumes,
scurry, having heard something, to take up their positions on
either side of the throne, with halberds raised. Four young
men dressed in eleventh-century German-knight costumes
burst in, talking:)*

LANDOLPH
(To BERTHOLD*)* "Ta-da" The throne room.

HAROLD
In some castle in Germany. Let's say—Goslar.

ORDULPH
Or Hartz maybe.

HAROLD
Or Wurms.

LANDOLPH
Depends. One minute here. The next—

ORDULPH
Saxony.

HAROLD
Lombardy!

LANDOLPH
On the Rhine!

FIRST SERVANT
(Standing very still) Excuse me...

HAROLD
What?

FIRST SERVANT
Isn't he coming?

ORDULPH
No. He's sleeping.

SECOND SERVANT
(Relaxing, to FIRST SERVANT*)* He could have told us.

FIRST SERVANT
(To HAROLD*)* Got a light?

LANDOLPH
No smoking in here.

FIRST SERVANT
(Taking HAROLD's *light)* A quickie.

BERTHOLD
I don't get it. Why a castle in Germany for the king of France?

LANDOLPH
King of France? Who said anything about the king of France?

ORDULPH
He thought he was the king of France? *(Laughs)*

HAROLD
Enrico IV of Germany. The Salian dynasty?

ORDULPH
The great and tragic emperor?

LANDOLPH
Canossa? In this room the church and state fight it out every day. Day in, day out. Rain or shine.

ORDULPH
Empire against the papacy!

HAROLD

Anti-popes versus the popes!

LANDOLPH

Kings versus against-the-kings!

ORDULPH

To hell with the Saxons!

HAROLD

To hell with the rebel princes!

LANDOLPH

To hell with the emperor's own sons!

BERTHOLD

I get it. I get it! So we're somewhere in the sixteenth century.

HAROLD

To hell with the sixteenth century!

ORDULPH

We're—what? Between a thousand and eleven hundred.

LANDOLPH

Figure it out: Canossa was in January 1077—

BERTHOLD

(To himself) Oh my god—

ORDULPH

He thought he was Enrico IV of France.

BERTHOLD

You wouldn't believe the books I've read—

LANDOLPH

No good to you now. We're four hundred years earlier.

BERTHOLD

Why the hell didn't someone tell me? For two weeks I've been reading the wrong books!

HAROLD

Tito played Adalbert of Bremen; you must have been
told that.

BERTHOLD

No.

LANDOLPH

So when Tito died—At first the marquis—

BERTHOLD

Why didn't he tell me?

HAROLD

He thought you knew!

LANDOLPH

(Continuing) At first the marquis didn't think he'd have
to replace poor Tito. That the three of us would be
enough. Then *he (Gestures off)* started screaming:
"They've taken my Adalbert!" See, he didn't know
Tito was dead, so he thought that the rival bishops
of Cologne and Mayence had—

BERTHOLD

I don't understand a word you're saying.

ORDULPH

That's not good.

HAROLD

Another problem is we don't know who you're
supposed to be.

BERTHOLD

What???

LANDOLPH

"They've taken my Adalbert! Get me Berthold! I want
Berthold!" That's all he said.

HAROLD

So you are—some Berthold. From the eleventh century.

LANDOLPH

But which one?

BERTHOLD

I'm getting out of here.

HAROLD

(Grabbing him) Hold on. Wait a minute.

LANDOLPH

It's not as bad as you think. None of us really knows
who he is. He's Harold. Ordulph. I'm Landolph.
It's what he calls us. But who are we? *(Shrugs)*
Names out of the eleventh century. Like—Berthold.
Only poor Tito had a decent part: he was Bishop of
Bremen. And he was a damn good Bishop of Bremen
too.

HAROLD

He worked hard at it.

LANDOLPH

One minute he'd be lecturing His Majesty, the next
counseling him—just like a bishop. We're the so-called
"secret counselors." That's all we know. You see, we
read—somewhere—that Enrico IV was disliked by
the aristocracy for surrounding himself with young
good-for-nothing sycophantic hangers-on.

ORDULPH

We think that must be us.

LANDOLPH

Good-for-nothings. Sponges. But always smiling.

BERTHOLD

Smiling??

HAROLD

All the time. Like us.

ORDULPH

It's not as easy as you think.

LANDOLPH

What's a shame is we could be so much more. We've
got the costumes. There's a lot of interesting drama in
Enrico's story, but we're given nothing to do. We're
like—props. We've been saying that the real hangers-
on had it a lot easier, at least they knew why they were
hangers-on, they must have had their reasons. What are
our reasons? Who knows? So we hang around and
wait. Hang around like a bunch of puppets on a wall,
waiting to be taken down, and moved around.

HAROLD

Waiting to be spoken to. And God help you if you say
the wrong thing.

LANDOLPH

True.

BERTHOLD

How the hell am I supposed to know what to say?
I've been studying the wrong Enrico!

HAROLD

Then you better start studying the right one right away.

ORDULPH

We can help.

HAROLD

We've got a whole library on the subject. But first the
main points.

ORDULPH

Good idea.

HAROLD

(Points to the paintings) There. What are they?

BERTHOLD

Uh...somewhat out of place modern-type paintings.
Two of them. Why are they here?

HAROLD

They haven't always been. There are two niches behind
them. They were going to put up two medieval statues,
but these went up instead.

LANDOLPH

Are you sure they're paintings?

BERTHOLD

What do you mean?

LANDOLPH

Touch them. To us—they are paintings and so seem out
of place in here, but to him...who never touches them....

BERTHOLD

To him what?

LANDOLPH

I'm guessing, but I think I'm right—to him, they're
reflections as if from a mirror. Understand? That one's
him, as Enrico IV, here, in this room. Close your mouth,
it's not that strange—if you looked in a mirror right
now what would you see—yourself dressed like that.
So for him, those are two mirrors reflecting the reality,
that you'll soon see, is lived here.

BERTHOLD

This is madness.

HAROLD

Not to us. We get paid.

BERTHOLD

So none of this—bothers you?

LANDOLPH

What if it did? What could we do? And if studying
history has taught us anything it's that it's best to keep
your mouth shut.

HAROLD

Come on, you'll soon get into it.

ORDULPH

Soon you'll be like us.

BERTHOLD

So what do I do? Give me the gist of the story anyway.

LANDOLPH

We'll hook on a few strings and turn him into a
first-rate puppet.

(They start to lead him off.)

BERTHOLD

(To the painting of the woman) You haven't told me who
that is—Enrico's wife?

HAROLD

No. The Emperor Enrico's wife is Bertha of Susa, the
sister of Amadeus II of Saxony.

ORDULPH

Enrico of course can't stand Bertha and wants to get rid
of her, or so he says to impress us young hangers-on.

LANDOLPH

(To the painting) She is his most ferocious enemy:
Matilda, Marchioness of Tuscany.

BERTHOLD

The one who took in the Pope?

LANDOLPH

Good for you! At Canossa.

ORDULPH

Pope Gregory VII.

HAROLD

Our great bogeyman. Let's go.

*(As they move to leave, JOHN, an elderly servant in
contemporary clothes, hurries in.)*

JOHN

Psst! Frank! Lolo!

HAROLD

What?

BERTHOLD

Who's he? Why isn't he dressed like us?

LANDOLPH

You're in the wrong century! Get out! Out!

(The others start teasing.)

ORDULPH

O messenger of Pope Gregory, away with thee!!

HAROLD

Be gone! Be gone!

JOHN

Stop it. Be quiet!

ORDULPH

Not one step more!

HAROLD

Out, I say! Out!

LANDOLPH

'Tis Black Magic! A Demon conjured up by the Wizard
of Room! Draw your swords, men!

(They pretend to draw their swords.)

JOHN

Stop it!! And grow up!! The marquis's arrived with
guests.

LANDOLPH

Any women?

ORDULPH

Any young women?

JOHN

There are two men.

HAROLD

Get to the women.

JOHN

The marchioness and her daughter.

LANDOLPH

(Surprised) What??

ORDULPH

The marchioness?

JOHN

Yes, the marchioness!

HAROLD

And the men?

JOHN

I don't know.

HAROLD

(Pretending again) Messengers from the pope!

ORDULPH

With messages from the pope!!

JOHN

Stop it! And that's the last time I'm telling you!

HAROLD

Sh-sh. Go ahead.

JOHN

One of the men's a doctor, I think.

LANDOLPH

Ah, another doctor.

HAROLD

Berthold, you've brought us luck!

LANDOLPH

Watch what we do to this doctor.

BERTHOLD

So we start already?

JOHN

Quiet. They want to come in here.

LANDOLPH

What? Here? The marchioness in here??

HAROLD

This is different. So we're out of the world of play-acting.

LANDOLPH

And into real-life drama?

BERTHOLD

What? Why?

ORDULPH

She—is her. *(Points to the painting)*

LANDOLPH

The daughter is the marquis's fiancé. But what's the mother doing here?

ORDULPH

If he sees her, there'll be big trouble.

LANDOLPH

If he even recognizes her.

JOHN

Still if he wakes up, keep him out of here.

ORDULPH

And how do you suggest we do that?

HAROLD

You know what he's like.

JOHN

Tie him up, I don't care! Those are my orders! Go! Go!

HAROLD

What if he's not asleep.

ORDULPH

Come on.

LANDOLPH

(To JOHN*)* Tell me later what's going on.

(They go.)

JOHN

(Shouting after them) Shut the door and hide the key!
That door too! *(To Young Servants)* You too. Get out.
And hide the key!

(They are gone. DONNA MATILDA, *her daughter,* FRIDA,
DR GENONI, BARON TITO BELCREDI, *and the young owner
of the house,* MARQUIS CHARLES DI NOLLI, *enter, speaking
in whispers:)*

DI NOLLI

(To JOHN*)* So we won't be "interrupted"?

JOHN

As you wished.

BELCREDI

Look at this! Incredible!

DOCTOR

Fascinating. The perfect setting to live out his delusions.

MATILDA

(Looks for her portrait and finds it.) Here it is. *(She goes to
the painting.)* Yes. Yes.

FRIDA

Your portrait.

MATILDA

No, look again. It's you.

(The painting looks very like FRIDA.*)*

DI NOLLI

Amazing resemblance, isn't it? See, I told you.

MATILDA

I wouldn't have believed it. *(She shivers.)* Spooky.
(Pulls her daughter aside.) Can't you see yourself?

FRIDA

I...I really...

MATILDA

It's you. Look closely. (To BELCREDI) Tito, tell her. Tito!

BELCREDI

I'm not going there. I'm not that dumb.

MATILDA

Idiot, I wouldn't be upset. (To DOCTOR) What about
you, Doctor? What do you think?

(He looks closely at the painting.)

BELCREDI

Careful, Doctor.

DOCTOR

Careful of what?

MATILDA

Don't listen to him. Come here. (To BELCREDI) I'm
getting so tired of you.

FRIDA

Always the clown.

BELCREDI

Watch your step, Doctor.

DOCTOR

My step?

BELCREDI

Or you'll end up with that foot in your mouth.

DOCTOR

(Trying to laugh) So the daughter looks like the mother
when the mother was young.

BELCREDI

Open wide!

DOCTOR

What? What's so odd about that!

BELCREDI

In it goes!

DOCTOR

I don't understand.

MATILDA

(Who hasn't heard the DOCTOR's *comment)* What did he say? Tell me.

DOCTOR

It's true, isn't it? For the daughter to look like the mother when the mother was young.

BELCREDI

The most common thing in the world. Nothing to get upset about.

MATILDA

(Upset) I'm not upset! That was me, not her, and now to see how much she looks like me, well, that is—odd. Fascinating. Nothing else.

FRIDA

Can't you two ever stop arguing?!

BELCREDI

(Apologetic) I understand now. *(To* FRIDA*)* You don't seem a bit surprised by how much you look like your mother. Or maybe you don't recognize her as your mother.

MATILDA

Why should she? It's not how she's ever known me. Whereas I can look at her and see myself at her age.

DOCTOR

This is interesting. The girl looks at this portrait and sees—herself? Just that. Like a reflection in a mirror. But the woman sees herself through the eyes of memory, and all sorts of things are conjured up, past gestures, fleeting glances, half smiles and so forth.

MATILDA

Yes. Yes they are.

DOCTOR

(Continuing) And then the woman looks at the girl in
life, and sees the same gestures, smiles, glances, but
they are no longer hers, no, now they are her daughter's.

MATILDA

"Thank you" for spelling that out.

DOCTOR

(To BELCREDI*)* Resemblance, I've found, has more often
to do with what one feels, than sees, with what one—

BELCREDI

All I know is that you're beginning to resemble me.
That's enough.

DI NOLLI

Yes, please, we're wasting time.

FRIDA

(Gestures toward BELCREDI*)* Blame him for that.

DI NOLLI

Please. We've asked the doctor here for a reason.
And we all know what that reason is.

DOCTOR

Exactly. So let's get started. First a few questions.
Marchioness, how did your portrait get here? At the
time of his accident, did you give it to him then?

MATILDA

No. How could I have? I was a girl, like Frida. I wasn't
even engaged. I gave it to him three or four years later.
His *(Points to* DI NOLLI*)* mother asked me for it. So I
gave it.

DOCTOR

(To DI NOLLI*)* Your mother was his sister?

DI NOLLI

Yes. May she rest in peace. It's because of her we're
now here. Frida and I had planned to be traveling
abroad.

DOCTOR

Therapy of another sort.

DI NOLLI

Mother died believing her brother was getting better.

DOCTOR

And why did she think that?

DI NOLLI

Because of things he said, strange things just before she
died.

DOCTOR

You wouldn't happen to recall any of these things?

DI NOLLI

I couldn't, sorry. All I know is that after her last visit
with him, Mother returned visibly excited. And just
before she died she made me promise to take care of
him, arrange for doctors to see him, and examine him.

DOCTOR

Uh-huh. Right. Good. Sometimes even the least—like
this portrait—

MATILDA

Doctor please, don't make too much out of that. I hadn't
seen it in years, that's why I reacted so—

DOCTOR

Please. Sh-sh. Sh-sh.

DI NOLLI

She hadn't seen it for what—fifteen years?

MATILDA

More, more, eighteen!

DOCTOR

I don't think you understand what I'm getting at: these
two portraits—could supply us with the key. A way in.
They were painted—obviously—before the famous and
unfortunate masquerade, weren't they?

MATILDA

Of course.

DOCTOR

So while he was still—sane. This is my point. Was it his idea to have the portraits made?

MATILDA

Lots of people had theirs done—as souvenirs.

BELCREDI

I had mine done—as Charles of Anjou!

MATILDA

(Continuing) Once our costumes were made.

BELCREDI

We talked of keeping them all together—as a sort of gallery after the masquerade, but everyone wanted to take his home.

MATILDA

And I gave him mine, it was the least I could do, when his (Gestures: DI NOLLI's) mother...

DOCTOR

But you don't know if he was the one who asked for it?

MATILDA

I suppose it could have just been his sister wanting to do something nice—

DOCTOR

One more thing: this masquerade, was it his idea?

BELCREDI

No, it was mine.

DOCTOR

Please—

MATILDA

Ignore him. It was poor Belassi's idea.

BELCREDI

Belassi? He had nothing to do with it.

MATILDA

Count Belassi, may he rest in peace, died two, three
months later—

BELCREDI

Belassi wasn't even there when—

DI NOLLI

Doctor, who cares whose idea it was?

DOCTOR

It could be important.

BELCREDI

It was mine, I'm telling you. Not that I'm proud of it,
considering... I'll tell you how it happened. I'm at the
club, this is early November, one evening, and I'm
thumbing through a German magazine. Looking at
the pictures, I can't read German. And I come across
a photo of the Kaiser in some town where he'd been a
student—

DOCTOR

Bonn. That was Bonn!

BELCREDI

Fine. Bonn. He's on a horse, dressed in one of those old
German student-guild costumes, and behind him's a
whole line of students, also in costume. That's how I got
the idea. We'd already been talking at the club about
having some sort of party, so I made the suggestion that
we put on a masquerade, with everyone choosing a
character—king, emperor, prince with a queen,
empress, princess with them, all arriving on horseback,
lit by torchlight. They loved it.

MATILDA

Belassi told me it was his idea.

BELCREDI

Then he lied. Belassi wasn't even at the club that night.
Nor was he (ENRICO).

DOCTOR

So he chose Enrico IV?

MATILDA

Because I'd chosen—for no reason at all—except the
name—the marchioness Matilda of Tuscany.

DOCTOR

I don't understand the connection.

MATILDA

Neither did I, in the beginning when he said he wished
to lie at my feet like Enrico IV at Canossa. The name
rang a bell from school, so I then looked up my
character's history and learned she'd been the close
friend and protector of Pope Gregory VII, the hated
enemy of Enrico. And that's when I understood why
he'd chosen to be Enrico beside my Matilda, because
to him, she was a woman who protected his enemies,
a woman who detested him.

DOCTOR

I see, because—

BELCREDI

Because he loved her. And she—what?

MATILDA

What?

BELCREDI

She couldn't stand him.

MATILDA

That's not true. I didn't dislike him. Not in the least!
But when a man decides he's serious about a woman—

BELCREDI

He risks looking like a fool.

MATILDA

That only goes for you.

BELCREDI

When am I ever serious?

MATILDA

I'd noticed. Anyway, you couldn't joke around with
him. Of all the burdens women must bear, Doctor, one
of the worst is to constantly confront a pair of wide
adoring eyes, radiating eternal devotion. *(Laughs)* I can't
help it, but I just laugh. If men could see how funny
they look. And it's always made me laugh, maybe less
now than then.... And so I laughed at him then, though
perhaps partly also out of fear—I can say that now after
twenty-odd years. I think I feared that he meant it, what
his eyes spoke. And for a girl—that can be frightening.

DOCTOR

Frightening? That's interesting.

MATILDA

He was different from the rest. And I was—and I
suppose still am—impatient with anyone who dares—
not to be frivolous. And then I was young, a woman—
so I knew no better. I hadn't the courage to be different.
So I laughed at him too—along with the rest, hating
myself, because I could see how much my laughter
hurt him.

BELCREDI

Sounds familiar.

MATILDA

Dear, you want people to laugh at you, God knows
why. He was different. The two aren't the same at all.
People laugh in your face.

BELCREDI

Better than behind my back.

DOCTOR

The facts: he was already then a bit different before the
accident.

BELCREDI

Yes. And in a very particular way.

DOCTOR

How?

BELCREDI

He seemed very aware of himself. As if watching
himself from somewhere else.

MATILDA

That makes him sound like a cold fish. He loved life.
He was just different from other people.

BELCREDI

Not cold—self-conscious. It was like he'd invented a
role for himself to play—which he then played with all
his heart. Though I think he felt frustrated, trapped by
it as well.

DOCTOR

(To MATILDA) What do you think?

MATILDA

I agree.

BELCREDI

And why? (To DOCTOR) Self-consciousness unchecked—
and now I speak from my own life—is soon a hall of
mirrors. You can watch yourself only for so long before
starting to wonder whether what you're watching is in
fact you or someone else. Pretty soon you're investing
your "character" with any feeling you think of—one
minute you're acting happy, then sad, then—on and
on until you don't know who the hell you really are or
how you feel about anything. And when you finally
stand back and take a good look: all you see is a
perfectly ridiculous man.

DOCTOR

And unsociable? Aloof?

BELCREDI

Not at all. He was always organizing things: dances,
benefits, concerts. Every sort of—show. Self-conscious
people are born actors.

DI NOLLI
And madness has made him an even better actor.

BELCREDI
He was always good. Take his accident. The horse fell—

DOCTOR
Hit his head, didn't he?

MATILDA
It was awful. I was riding next to him. I saw him under
his horse's hooves. The horse reared—!

BELCREDI
He appeared fine. Though everyone wanted to make
sure, and the party stopped for a bit, at least until he
was helped inside.

MATILDA
There was no wound. Not a drop of blood.

BELCREDI
We thought he'd had the wind knocked out of him.

MATILDA
Then a couple of hours later—

BELCREDI
I'm telling this. He returned to the party—

MATILDA
When I saw his face, I knew what had happened.

BELCREDI
No you didn't. Not one of us did. That's my point.

MATILDA
How could you know? (To DOCTOR) They were
behaving like crazy people.

BELCREDI
We were still in our costumes. We were pretending to
be our characters.

MATILDA
But he wasn't pretending, Doctor. It was terrible—

DOCTOR

So he returned to the party, still dressed as—

BELCREDI

Yes. He seemed fine, played along like the rest of
us—maybe better. As I said, he could act.

MATILDA

Someone teased him, tickled him with a fan as he
walked by—

BELCREDI

And he pulled out his sword, as an emperor he had a
sword, and began swinging it at us. For real. A real
sword!

MATILDA

I'll never forget it—we were still in our masks, terrified
and screaming, while there he was, mask off now, with
a face contorted into something—unnatural.

BELCREDI

He was Enrico IV. He'd become Enrico IV.

MATILDA

He'd been studying him for weeks, and so that's what
came out.

DOCTOR

Because of the fall, which damaged the brain. He
became what he was pretending to be when he hit his
head.

BELCREDI

(To FRIDA and DI NOLLI) You see, children, how you can
never predict what life has in store. (To DI NOLLI) You
were what—four or five then? (To FRIDA) And you
weren't even a thought and certainly not the woman
your mother sees in her portrait. And look at my grey
hair. But him—one hit on the head and he's stuck in
time—Enrico IV forever!

DOCTOR

If I may give an opinion—

(Door bursts open and BERTHOLD *hurries in, startling everyone.)*

BERTHOLD

I'm sorry. Sorry.

FRIDA

It's him!

MATILDA

Oh god, is it?!

DI NOLLI

No it isn't! Get a hold of yourselves.

DOCTOR

Who is it then?

BELCREDI

An actor?

DI NOLLI

One of the young men I've hired to help him.

BERTHOLD

I'm sorry to interrupt, sir—

DI NOLLI

Didn't I say we didn't want to be disturbed in here?!

BERTHOLD

Yes, but I thought I should tell you that I'm quitting.
(Turns to go.)

DI NOLLI

Wait. Are you the one who started this morning?

BERTHOLD

Yes. And one morning's plenty for me.

MATILDA

Then he's worse than you've said.

BERTHOLD

No, no it's not him. It's the others. The ones you say
you've hired to help him. They're crazy.

(LANDOLPH *and* HAROLD *enter.)*

LANDOLPH

Excuse us.

HAROLD

May we come in, sir?

DI NOLLI

Come in. What's wrong? What's going on?

FRIDA

I don't like this, I'm getting out of here.

DI NOLLI

(Stopping her) No, you're not.

LANDOLPH

Sir this—boy here (BERTHOLD)—

BERTHOLD

I told you I quit!

LANDOLPH

You're not going anywhere.

HAROLD

Sir, the boy's done something to make him (ENRICO)
angry. So he wants the boy arrested and plans to try
him here from the throne. We can't keep him out much
longer. What do we do?

DI NOLLI

Close the door. Close the door! And that one!

HAROLD

Ordulph alone can't keep him out.

LANDOLPH

What if we announce the guests—get him thinking of
something else? Have you worked out why you're here?

DI NOLLI

We talked about it. *(To* DOCTOR*)* Should we wait or see
him now, Doctor?

FRIDA

I don't want to be a part of this. Mother, let's get out of
here.

DOCTOR

He's not—armed is he?

DI NOLLI

Of course not! *(To* FRIDA*)* Frida, don't be a baby, you
wanted to come.

FRIDA

I didn't, Mother did.

MATILDA

And I'm ready to see him. So what do we do?

BELCREDI

We don't have to dress up, do we?

LANDOLPH

Absolutely. God knows what he'd do if he saw
someone dressed like that. *(Gestures)*

HAROLD

He might think it was some trick.

DI NOLLI

In his eyes, we're in the funny clothes.

LANDOLPH

By his mortal enemy.

BELCREDI

Pope Gregory VII?

LANDOLPH

The one he calls the pagan pope.

BELCREDI

"Pagan pope"—I like that.

LANDOLPH

As well as "infidel" and the devil himself.
He's obsessed with him.

DOCTOR

Paranoia.

HAROLD

Who knows what he'd do.

DI NOLLI

(To BELCREDI*)* Though there's no reason for you to stay,
the doctor can see him alone.

DOCTOR

What do you mean—alone?

DI NOLLI

They'll *(The young men)* be here.

DOCTOR

I thought Donna Matilda—

MATILDA

I do. I wish to see him too. Again.

FRIDA

Mother, please, get out of here!

MATILDA

Stop it. I came here for a reason. *(To* LANDOLPH*)* I shall
be "Adelaide," his mother-in-law.

LANDOLPH

Very good. Empress Bertha's mother. All you'll need is
a cloak to cover your clothes and a crown. Harold, get
them.

HAROLD

What about him *(The* DOCTOR*)*?

DOCTOR

We thought I'd be—the bishop of Cluny, Hugh of
Cluny.

LANDOLPH

He comes here a lot.

DOCTOR

What do you mean?

LANDOLPH
Don't worry, it's a nice disguise.

HAROLD
We use it all the time.

DOCTOR
But—

LANDOLPH
He won't notice. He only looks at the costume, not the
face.

MATILDA
That's good for me too.

DI NOLLI
Frida, we'll wait outside. Come on, Tito.

BELCREDI
No, if she's here, I'm here.

MATILDA
But I don't need you here.

BELCREDI
Maybe you don't, but I still want to see him for myself.
Is that a problem?

LANDOLPH
Maybe three's better, more official.

HAROLD
What's he going to wear?

BELCREDI
You must have something...

LANDOLPH
Let me think. Fine. You'll be from Cluny too.

BELCREDI
What does that mean?

LANDOLPH
A monk. Who's come with him (DOCTOR). (To HAROLD)
Go. (To BERTHOLD) And you stay out of sight. No, wait.

(To HAROLD*)* Give him *(*BERTHOLD*)* the costumes,
and you go announce the arrival of "Duchess Adelaide"
and "The Bishop of Cluny." Go!

*(*HAROLD *and* BERTHOLD *hurry off.)*

DI NOLLI

We better leave.

(He leaves with FRIDA.*)*

DOCTOR

Does—he—"like" the bishop of Cluny?

LANDOLPH

Are you kidding? But don't worry about that. The
bishop has always been treated pretty well here.
And you too, my lady. He has never forgotten that
it was because of the help of you two that he was
admitted to the castle of Canossa and into the presence
of Pope Gregory VII, who then wouldn't receive him.

BELCREDI

And what about me? What do I do?

LANDOLPH

Stand there. That's it.

MATILDA

(To BELCREDI*)* I wish you'd go.

BELCREDI

You seem—excited.

MATILDA

I am. Leave me alone.

*(*BERTHOLD *returns with the costumes.)*

LANDOLPH

The costumes are here. The cloak's for the lady—

MATILDA

Shouldn't I take my hat off? *(She does.)*

LANDOLPH

(To BERTHOLD*)* Give it to him. *(Holds up the crown,
to* MATILDA*)* Try this.

MATILDA

Is there a mirror?

LANDOLPH

Through there. Would you rather put it on yourself?

MATILDA

Do you mind? Thank you.

(She takes her hat, and BERTHOLD *follows with the cloak
and crown.)*

BELCREDI

I never thought I'd end up a Benedictine monk.
These clothes aren't cheap.

DOCTOR

What fantasy is?

BELCREDI

Good thing he's rich.

LANDOLPH

We have a whole wardrobe full of period costumes
perfectly copied from books. This is one of my jobs—
to hire the costume designers and no, they don't come
cheap.

*(*MATILDA *returns, wearing cloak and crown.)*

BELCREDI

Fantastic. Like a real queen.

MATILDA

(Laughing at BELCREDI*)* Take that off. Please. You look
ridiculous. You look like an ostrich.

BELCREDI

How about him *(The* DOCTOR*)*?

MATILDA

He's all right. It's just you.

DOCTOR

Does he have a lot of guests?

LANDOLPH

I suppose. Sometimes he sends for—"so-and-so." So—
we have to go out and get somebody to be "so-and-so."
Sometimes he—wants a woman.

MATILDA

A woman?

LANDOLPH

Not as often now.

BELCREDI

What sort of woman—in costume, like her?

LANDOLPH

A woman who'll do what she's asked.

BELCREDI

Ah. *(To* MATILDA*)* Watch your step.

(Door opens, HAROLD *enters and announces)*

HAROLD

His Majesty the Emperor Enrico IV!

*(*ENRICO *enters between* ORDULPH *and* HAROLD. *He wears
a penitent's sack over his royal costume.* ORDULPH *carries
the crown, and* HAROLD *the scepter with eagle and globe
with cross. His hair has been badly colored, on his cheeks two
doll-like circles of rouge. He bows to* MATILDA, *then to the*
DOCTOR.*)*

ENRICO

My lady... *(To* DOCTOR*)* Bishop...*(He notices* BELCREDI,
starts to greet him, then stops and turns to LANDOLPH *and
whispers)* Peter Damiani?

LANDOLPH

No, sire. A monk from Cluny accompanying the bishop.

(He stares at BELCREDI, *then finally:)*

ENRICO

Peter Damiani. You can't fool me. *(Turning quickly to*
MATILDA*)* You have my word, I swear I now love your
daughter. It's true I tried to divorce her and would have
succeeded had not he (BELCREDI*)* come in the name
of Pope Alexander and forbidden it. The bishop of
Mayence was all set to do it too—for a mere hundred
and twenty farms. *(Turns to* LANDOPLH*)* But enough
about the integrity of bishops. *(To* BELCREDI*)* Thank
God you stopped me and prevented yet another
mistake in a lifetime of mistakes: my mother, Adalbert,
Tribur, Goslar! And now this sackcloth! *(To himself,*
as almost a mantra) Look up, stand up straight, breathe.
(To them) I'm well versed in humiliation now. I can even
humiliate myself before you (BELCREDI*)*, Bishop Peter
Damiani. *(Bows, then suddenly turns on him:)* You better
not be the one spreading the rumor about my mother
sleeping with the pope.

BELCREDI

No, I—

ENRICO

I didn't think so. I didn't think you'd have the guts.
(To DOCTOR, *about* BELCREDI*)* What do I always say
about bishops?

HAROLD

(Cueing the DOCTOR*)* Can't trust those bishops.

DOCTOR

Can't trust those—

ENRICO

Greedy bastards. Six years old and king but I'm still
six years old. They tore me from my mother and used
me—to hurt her. The sons of bitches, they'd steal the
shirt off your back. Each one greedier than the next.
Anno's got his hand in Stephan's pocket. Stephan's
got his in Anno's—

LANDOLPH

Sire...

ENRICO

Enough about bishops. But these slanders about my
mother, they upset me. *(To* MATILDA*)* I can't even
mourn her, you know. As a mother yourself, imagine
that. She was here only last month. From her convent.
Now I'm told she's dead. *(Pause)* I cannot mourn
because if you are here and I am dressed like this,
then I am twenty-six.

HAROLD

And she is still alive.

ORDULPH

In her convent.

ENRICO

So I must mourn—later. *(Suddenly shows* MATILDA *his
dyed hair.)* Look here: youth. *(To* DOCTOR*)* You've got
nothing to worry about—yet. You don't need help—
yet. *(To* MATILDA*)* But you—what color are your roots?
I'm not criticizing. We're all the same. Who wants to
grow old? I didn't. But what choice do we have in these
matters, what choice do we have in anything? So it's
best, isn't it to—accept.

DOCTOR

Yes. That's true, very true.

ENRICO

Accept who we are, because if we don't—who are we?
(To MATILDA*)* A woman trying to be a man?
(To BELCREDI*)* An old man trying to be young?
How silly. *(To* DOCTOR*)* Or do you just choose a role?
A comfortable way you'd like to see yourself, or have
the world see you—and never for an instant step out of
it, while all the time holding tight to say your bishop's
clothes, and not noticing that falling out of your sleeve,
peeling off your back like a snake's skin is something
you've forgotten all about: life. *(To* MATILDA*)* Have you

never been surprised by yourself, my lady? Surprised
to learn that you were not the person you thought you
were? Haven't you ever done something, treated
someone in some way that made you say—but that's
not really me. I'm not like that. Haven't you? Think.

(*She nearly faints.*)

ENRICO

You have? Your secret's safe with me. And you, Peter
Damiani, to be such a person's friend!

LANDOLPH

Majesty...

ENRICO

I name no names! (*To* BELCREDI) What is your opinion
of such a person? But then who doesn't cling to some
image we have of ourselves, just as who doesn't dye
his hair? Now others may see right through you, but
I don't dye my hair for others, I dye it because this
is how I see me. You, you, my lady, are obviously
deceiving no one, not even yourself. No, your dyed hair
deceives only that image in the mirror. But for you it's
serious, for me—fun. We all wear our costumes, though
some of us more seriously than others. I don't mean
that crown and cloak either, rather the memories we
wear of how once we were but are no more—fair and
beautiful? Or was it dark? Your costume's the worn
and faded memory of your youth. (*Turns to* BELCREDI)
Whereas Peter Damiani here, for you it's different.
You have no memories to dress up in. You've forgotten
who you were and why you did what you did, so life's
a blur lived amidst a dream. Me too. So much of my life
doesn't make sense too—like dreams. Oh well. Peter
Damiani, such is our luck. And tomorrow won't be any
better. (*Grabs hold of the sackcloth*) This sackcloth...

(*Struggles to get it off, the young men hurry to help him.*)

ENRICO

I can do it!

(They back away. He gets the sackcloth off.)

ENRICO

Tomorrow, at Fressanone, twenty-seven German and
Lombard bishops will join with me in demanding the
removal of Gregory VII. He's no pope! He's a conniving
monk!

ORDULPH

Sire. Majesty, please—

HAROLD

The bishop and the duchess are here to intercede on
your behalf.

(Gestures to the DOCTOR *to say something.)*

DOCTOR

That's right. We are.

ENRICO

(Suddenly apologizing) Forgive me. Sir. Forgive me,
please, my lady. It's the stress of being under this
threat of excommunication. *(To* HAROLD *and* ORDULPH*)*
Why can't I humble myself before that man?

LANDOLPH

Majesty, we've told you he is not Peter Damiani.

ENRICO

He isn't?

HAROLD

No, he's just a poor monk, Majesty.

ENRICO

Then I assumed too much without thinking. Something
you can appreciate, madam, as a woman. Your
daughter—Bertha, my wife—I swear I now love her—
I swear it! And she has earned my love through her
devotion and affection during these trying times.
You must know that she came after me, traveling like
a beggar, sleeping outside in the snow. You are her
mother. Doesn't that touch a mother's heart? Show us

your pity and beg His Holiness for a pardon, beg him to
receive us.

MATILDA

Yes, of course.

DOCTOR

We promise!

ENRICO

And one more thing! It's not enough for him just to
receive us. He has the power to do—anything. Even
raise the dead. (*He touches his chest.*) Here I am. I stand
before you. There is nothing—no magic—out of his
reach. So sir, my lady, I live under a curse, and there
it is. (*Points to his portrait*) I am humble, humility itself,
and so shall I be before him. But when I have received
his forgiveness, won't you also get him to do this one
thing—remove the curse, cut me free from that (*The
painting*). Let me live out my miserable life in peace.
We cannot be twenty-six forever. My lady, I ask this for
your daughter's sake as well, so I may love her as she
deserves to be loved. That's it. I've said it. My fate lies
in your hands. Bishop. My lady.

(*He bows and leaves.* MATILDA *begins to sob.*)

END OF ACT ONE

ACT TWO

(*Another room in the villa, adjoining the "throne room" of ACT ONE. Late afternoon, the same day.*)

(MATILDA, *the* DOCTOR, *and* BELCREDI; *the latter two are in the middle of conversation.*)

BELCREDI

Maybe. But I don't think so.

DOCTOR

It's just an impression.

BELCREDI

I think he believes every word. (*To* MATILDA) Don't you?

MATILDA

What? Oh. Yes. But not in the way you think.

DOCTOR

He saw right through our costumes. But pretended not to—like a child play-acting.

MATILDA

A child? What are you talking about?

DOCTOR

In one sense, that is what he is: a big child. But it's also a lot more complicated than that.

MATILDA

What's complicated? I understood him perfectly.

DOCTOR

We must remember that the insane have a particular
psychology of their own: while they may detect that
someone is disguised, they can still believe in that
disguise. Much as children do when they play and
pretend that their fantasy is reality. That's why I
say in one sense he's a child, but it is of course more
complicated because what he's pretending to be—is an
image of what he once was. And that's the image in that
painting.

BELCREDI

He talked about that.

DOCTOR

So... We walk into here, in our costumes, and stand
before his image of himself. In his perfectly lucid
delirium he can tell the difference: That we don't belong
with that painted image. So he's suspicious, as all
madmen are. But his suspicions don't prevent him
from continuing to pretend with us—to play—so
though from our point of view he may appear—sad,
even tragic—from his own, he's simply having fun.
Pretending. Which explains the hair and painted cheeks
and that talk about for him it's all a joke.

MATILDA

That's not it. That's not it at all.

DOCTOR

What is it then, may I ask?

MATILDA

I am certain that he recognized me.

DOCTOR

That's not possible—

BELCREDI

(At the same time) How could he?!

MATILDA

I'm sure he did. When he got close to me and looked
me in the eyes—I knew he recognized me.

BELCREDI

He was talking to you as the mother of his wife.

MATILDA

That's not true! He was talking to me! Me!

BELCREDI

Who knows, maybe—

MATILDA

When he said that about my dyed hair, remember—he
added "or was it dark?" I had dark hair. Black hair.

BELCREDI

So what?

MATILDA

Doctor, my hair is naturally dark—so is my daughter's.
That's why he kept talking about my daughter.

BELCREDI

Which daughter?! He's never seen your real daughter!

MATILDA

Exactly! You are so stupid. What he said about my
daughter—he meant me. About me *then*!

BELCREDI

This is crazy, this is really crazy.

MATILDA

Shut up.

BELCREDI

One question: Have you ever been his wife? Because
your "daughter" is his wife—in his delirium she's
Bertha of Susa, Enrico IV's wife!

MATILDA

Right! And since I'm no longer dark—as he remembers
me—but "light-colored," I pretended to be "Adelaide,"

the mother. My daughter—either daughter—real or not
real—neither, as you've just said, ever existed for him,
so how does he know she's fair or dark?

BELCREDI

Maybe he meant "dark" in—sort of a general way.
He was covering all the possibilities: fair-haired,
dark-haired, it was the youthful memory he was talking
about! What is your problem? And Doctor you were
worried about my being in there, what about her?

MATILDA

He was speaking to me. Everything he said was to me,
about me, for me—

BELCREDI

Oh really?! And all that stuff to me, what was that?
Or maybe what he said about Peter Damiani was about
you too?!

MATILDA

In a way, maybe. Or do you have another explanation
for why, from the beginning, he showed such a strong
dislike of you.

(Silence)

DOCTOR

That could be explained by having had only the visit
of the duchess Adelaide and the bishop of Cluny
announced, and then a third person in there. So he
was suspicious...

BELCREDI

Of course. And being suspicious he saw me as an
enemy: Peter Damiani. But no, for her it's got to be:
"He's recognized me!"

MATILDA

He did. I could read it in his eyes. You know that
feeling...perhaps it was only for an instant, but for
at least that instant—I am sure he knew me.

DOCTOR

Not impossible: a lucid moment—

MATILDA

See?! And then he spoke with such regret for his
youth—and mine—and of that horrible thing that
happened to him, and that has kept him here, locked
inside a masquerade from which he can't escape, from
which he longs to be free.

BELCREDI

And to run into the daughter's arms—or, your arms, is
that what you think—having been freed by your pity?

MATILDA

Of which there is a great deal.

BELCREDI

More than seems appropriate actually.

DOCTOR

May I speak? As I've explained before, what I was
looking to discover was the flexibility of his delusion
or rather its intransigence. So I listened very closely
to everything he said. In my opinion, he seems subject
to sudden thoughts, perhaps recollections, (*Turns to*
MATILDA) perhaps fleeting memories as you say, which
at least for an instant relaxed the delirium. In other
words, he seemed, at times, to be listening to us, and
reacting to us not as props in his play, but as people in
the same room. Only moments, perhaps only fleeting,
but still promising, comforting, even as they show a
vigorous mental activity, a life inside the mind that
perhaps we can reach. So it's very possible that a jolt,
such as we have discussed, could very well—

MATILDA

Where is that car? It's been three and a half hours—

DOCTOR

What? Were you listening—?

MATILDA

The car. It's been more than three and a half—

DOCTOR

(*Looking at his watch*) More than four hours.

MATILDA

It would have been back ages ago.

BELCREDI

Maybe they couldn't find the dress—

MATILDA

I explained exactly where it was. And Frida? Where's
Frida?

BELCREDI

(*Looking out the window*) Maybe in the garden with
Charles.

DOCTOR

He'll keep her together.

BELCREDI

She's really not afraid, trust me. She's just fed up with
the whole thing.

MATILDA

Just don't pressure her. That won't get you anywhere.

DOCTOR

Patience. We have to wait until it's dark anyway, and
then—it'll be over in a second. One quick sudden shock
to jolt him out of these delusions, and break forever the
chains—already weakened—which bind him to his
fiction, and we give him what he longs for. Remember
what he said, "We can't be twenty-six forever, my
lady." We free him from this hell, which even he knows
is hell, and hopefully to reenter the world of today—

BELCREDI

(*Ironically*) He'll be cured! We'll have saved him!

DOCTOR

We hope, like a stopped watch, that we'll get ticking
again. A little shake, and—let's hope it starts up again.

(DI NOLLI *enters.*)

MATILDA

Charles, where's Frida?!

DI NOLLI

She's coming.

DOCTOR

Is the car here?

DI NOLLI

Yes.

MATILDA

Did they find the dress?

DI NOLLI

It's been here for a while.

DOCTOR

Good. Very good!

MATILDA

Where is she? Where's my daughter?

DI NOLLI

She's coming, she's coming.

(*Door opens.*)

DI NOLLI

Here she comes.

(BERTHOLD *enters to announce:*)

BERTHOLD

Her Highness the Countess Matilda of Canossa!

(FRIDA *enters in the same dress her mother wore for the
portrait and looking now like the painting come to life.*)

FRIDA
(Passing BERTHOLD and correcting) And also of Tuscany!
Canossa's just one of my many castles.

BELCREDI
(Stunned) My God, look at her.

MATILDA
She's—me. She's my picture come to life.

DOCTOR
Exactly. It's perfect: the picture lives.

BELCREDI
It's true. She is the picture. Fantastic.

FRIDA
Don't make me laugh or I'll bust out of this. I can't
believe the waist you had. I could barely squeeze
myself in.

MATILDA
(Fussing) Stop. Keep still. These pleats... Is it really tight
on you?

FRIDA
I can't breathe. Let's get this over with.

DOCTOR
We have to wait until it's dark.

FRIDA
Dark? I can't hold out that long.

MATILDA
Why didn't you wait to put it on?

FRIDA
I couldn't help myself.

MATILDA
You could have at least called me to help. It's all
wrinkled.

FRIDA
They were already there. I couldn't get them out.

DOCTOR

A few wrinkles don't matter. It's perfect. Just
move—there. A little farther. There.

BELCREDI

(*Comparing*) The world then—the world today.

MATILDA

What twenty years has done.

BELCREDI

Not as much as you think.

MATILDA

I meant the dress, I didn't mean—

BELCREDI

Speaking of the dress, Doctor, we're not talking twenty
years, but eight hundred. An abyss. Quite the jump
from there (FRIDA) to there (MATILDA). You'll have to
scrape him up off the ground. (*Laughs, others don't.*)
Serious, what I meant is that for us it's a couple of
dresses, a masquerade, twenty years, but for him, if as
you say time has stopped, and he lives (*Points to* FRIDA)
eight hundred years ago... (*Stops himself, then digging
himself deeper:*) I suppose what I was trying to say was:
a jump of that distance, anyone's bound to get a little
light-headed—

(DOCTOR *shakes his head.*)

BELCREDI

Then what do you think?

DOCTOR

That life goes on. And this—our life—will take a hold
of him and wrestle from him his illusions and expose
the distance traveled to be not eight hundred, but only
twenty years. We need only to get him to leap—and the
rest will follow. It's not unlike the Masonic rite where
the initiate, blindfolded, must leap off a ledge into the
blank unknown, when in fact he's but a step off the
ground.

BELCREDI

I've just had an incredible thought. Look at those two
(FRIDA *and* MATILDA). Which—is the more stylish?
The more modern? The more contemporary? The
young one? No. Us older people. Oh the young ones
think they are, think they're really—vogue, but we're
way past them, we're years ahead.

DOCTOR

So what are you saying?

BELCREDI

Look at those two (FRIDA *and* DI NOLLI). They have
their lives ahead of them: to grow old, to make the
same stupid mistakes, more or less, that we've made.
My point is that when we enter the world, we start—
at zero, and spend the rest of our lives catching up.
And if you follow that thought, then Adam, say, the
first man, were he alive, would be the most stylish of us
all. The most—advanced. And her — (FRIDA) —she's
eight hundred years ahead of us!

DI NOLLI

To you everything's a joke.

BELCREDI

I'm not joking now.

DI NOLLI

Ever since you arrived—

BELCREDI

What are you talking about? I put on these monk's
clothes, didn't I?

DI NOLLI

For a serious purpose.

BELCREDI

I know that. But I'm not the only one. Frida was making
fun—(*To* DOCTOR) You know, I still don't have the
faintest idea what you want to do.

DOCTOR

(Annoyed) You'll see. Just watch. The marchioness has yet to change—

BELCREDI

She has to dress up too?

DOCTOR

They've found something here, close to that *(FRIDA's dress)*—so he'll see two Countess Matildas of Canossa.

FRIDA

And of Tuscany! Don't forget Tuscany!

DOCTOR

What does that have to do with anything?

BELCREDI

So he's faced with both worlds at—

DOCTOR

Exactly.

FRIDA

Doctor, could we talk to you?

DOCTOR

Of course.

(He goes to FRIDA and DI NOLLI.)

BELCREDI

(To MATILDA) You're not worried that this is getting out of hand?

MATILDA

What?

BELCREDI

Are you really going to go through with this?

MATILDA

If it could help him...

BELCREDI

Bullshit! Why are you doing this to me?

MATILDA

What are you talking about?

BELCREDI

How am I supposed to feel as you "display" yourself?!

MATILDA

Who cares how you feel?

DI NOLLI

Fine. That's what we'll do. *(To* BERTHOLD*)* You, go and get one of the men.

*(*BERTHOLD *hurries off.)*

MATILDA

First, we have to pretend we're leaving.

DI NOLLI

Right. That's what I'm doing. *(To* BELCREDI*)* You don't mind staying behind?

BELCREDI

Oh don't worry about me.

DI NOLLI

It'll seem less suspicious.

BELCREDI

Treat me like I'm not even here. "Where's Tito, anyone seen Tito?"

DI NOLLI

He must be convinced we've left.

*(*LANDOLPH *enters with* BERTHOLD*.)*

LANDOLPH

Should I come in?

DI NOLLI

You, you're—Lol, aren't you?

LANDOLPH

Lolo. Landolph.

DI NOLLI

The doctor and the marchioness are leaving right away.

LANDOLPH

Fine. We just have to say they've got the pope to meet
him. He's in his room feeling pretty awful about
everything he said before, he's convinced he'll never
get the pope's pardon. (To DOCTOR) Could you tell him
yourself? It'll just take a minute. You'll have to put the
cloak back on.

DOCTOR

Of course. I don't mind.

LANDOLPH

Might I also suggest that you say that it was the
marchioness Matilda who got the pope to agree?

MATILDA

The marchioness???

LANDOLPH

Wasn't Enrico secretly in love with the marchioness of
Tuscany?

MATILDA

There's no historical proof of that. None.

LANDOLPH

We couldn't find any either. But he says he loves her.
He says it all the time. And now he's worried that his
secret love has only made her hate him more, and so
works against him with the pope.

MATILDA

We must let him know she no longer hates him.

LANDOLPH

Very good. Of course.

MATILDA

(To BELCREDI) According to history—I'll bet you didn't
know this—it was the marchioness Matilda, along with
the bishop of Cluny, who convinced the pope to meet

Enrico. Twenty years ago, I'd hoped to use this fact at the masquerade, as a way of showing how I truly felt about him.

BELCREDI
I hadn't realized you were such a stickler for historical detail.

LANDOLPH
Then why don't you see him now as the marchioness of Tuscany with the bishop—

DOCTOR
No! No! That would ruin everything. It needs to come as a shock, like I've said. No, you're still Duchess Adelaide, the mother of his wife. And then—we leave. That's very important, that he thinks we've left. Come on, we've wasted enough time, there's a lot to do.

(DOCTOR, MATILDA, and LANDOLPH leave.)

FRIDA
I'm beginning to get scared again.

DI NOLLI
Again?

FRIDA
It's just that I haven't even seen what he looks like.

DI NOLLI
He's nothing to be scared about.

FRIDA
Does he look crazy?

DI NOLLI
No, he's quite calm.

BELCREDI
And melancholy. Didn't you hear, he secretly loves you.

FRIDA
Thank you, that's what scares me.

BELCREDI

He won't hurt you.

DI NOLLI

It'll be over before you know it.

FRIDA

Still, in the dark, with a crazy man...

DI NOLLI

For a second. And I'll be there. They'll all be in the next room ready to run in. As soon as he sees your mother, your part's done.

BELCREDI

The one who scares me is this so-called doctor.

DI NOLLI

Stop it. It's going to work.

FRIDA

It is sort of exciting.

BELCREDI

There's just one thing about madmen you seem to be forgetting.

DI NOLLI

And what's that?

BELCREDI

They are mad.

DI NOLLI

What do you mean?

BELCREDI

He sees her. He sees her mother. Logically that should confuse him. Even shock him. But why should a madman be logical?

DI NOLLI

Logic has nothing to do with it.

BELCREDI

I'm beginning to see that.

DI NOLLI

He'll see his own delusion—in double. As the doctor
says.

BELCREDI

There's another thing—why are these people called
"doctor"?

FRIDA

What should they be called?

BELCREDI

I'll think of something.

BERTHOLD

(Who's been waiting at the door) There they are, I see
them. They're—on their way here.

DI NOLLI

Here?

BERTHOLD

He's with them. He's coming. He's coming!

DI NOLLI

Get out. Everyone out. *(To* BERTHOLD*)* You stay here.

BERTHOLD

Do I have to?

*(*DI NOLLI, FRIDA, BELCREDI *hurry out, leaving* BERTHOLD
alone as the others, MATILDA, *the* DOCTOR, *and* ENRICO
enter, with ORDULPH *and* HAROLD *behind them.)*

ENRICO

(In the middle of conversation) So which is it: Am I
calculating or just stupid?

DOCTOR

I would never call you stupid.

ENRICO

So—calculating.

DOCTOR

Neither stupid nor calculating.

ENRICO

Really? Since you can't be both I'd hoped for
calculating. At least that's useful. But I suppose
you're keeping that for yourself.

DOCTOR

Me? Do I seem calculating to you?

ENRICO

No. No, you don't. And perhaps there's the proof of
my stupidity. (To MATILDA) Could we talk in private?
(Takes her aside) Do you love your daughter?

MATILDA

Yes, certainly, I—

ENRICO

So I should shower her with my love and devotion to
make amends for all the wrongs I've done her—by the
way, don't believe everything my enemies say, I'm not
as debauched as all that.

MATILDA

No, I don't believe them. I've never believed those
stories.

ENRICO

So it's what you want?

MATILDA

(Confused) What??

ENRICO

That I go back to loving your daughter. (He looks at her,
then gives a mysterious warning:) Don't trust the
marchioness of Tuscany.

MATILDA

I've told you already she's done more than we have to
get the pope to—

ENRICO

I don't want to know. Stop. I can't think about her.

MATILDA

You still love her?

ENRICO

Who told you that? No one knows! No one could know!

MATILDA

Maybe she knows and that's why she tries so hard to
help.

(She looks away, then)

ENRICO

So you say you love your daughter. *(To* DOCTOR,
laughing) Well, I don't. Let it be a sin, but I feel nothing
for her. Strange, neither does her own mother. Say it,
my lady, she means very little to you. *(To* DOCTOR*)*
She won't stop about that woman. On and on and
on—Why?!! Why?!!

LANDOLPH

Maybe, Majesty, she's just trying to correct a
misimpression you have about the marchioness of
Tuscany. *(Corrects himself)* A misimpression you have
at this moment, I mean.

ENRICO

You too think she's trying to help me?

LANDOLPH

Yes. Right now she is.

MATILDA

That's true. That's so true.

ENRICO

I see. But you don't believe that I love her. That I—want
her. Nobody does. Probably for the best. That's enough
of that. *(To* DOCTOR*)* Bishop, you see that whether my
excommunication is revoked or not will have nothing
to do with "higher principles." Tell Gregory I'll meet
him again at Brixen. And you, my lady, should you
happen to run across your daughter in, say, the
courtyard of the castle of her dear friend Matilda, tell

her I want to see her. Let's see what she does for me,
my wife and empress. A lot of women claim to be
her—I sleep with most of them. It's not a sin, if she's
your wife. They're Bertha from Susa, they say, and then
start giggling. Shy? *(Confidentially)* This always happens
in bed. Yes? Under the sheets. Naked. A man and a
woman. What could be more—natural? Like so—who
cares who we are? Our clothes hanging in the corner—
like ghosts. *(To* DOCTOR*)* And ghosts, Bishop, are the
confusions of our souls. What can't be slept away.
They hover near us and frighten us—especially at
night when they climb off their horses, laughing,
approaching. Sometimes I'm even frightened of the
beat of my own heart in the silence of the night, like
footsteps in distant empty rooms. But enough of that.
I've kept you standing here far too long. My lady.
Bishop.

*(*MATILDA *and the* DOCTOR *go off bowing.)*

*(*ENRICO *is suddenly changed.)*

ENRICO

Idiots! What do they take me for? I can get them to say
anything! And the other one—"Damiani"? I had him
pegged from the start. That clown couldn't even look
me in the eye. *(Points to* BERTHOLD*.)* Look at him—his
mouth's hanging open. *(Shakes him)* Don't you get it!
Don't you see what I'm doing? They think I'm crazy,
so I'm having a little fun. *(To the others)* What's wrong
with that? It wasn't my idea for them to get dressed up
like that.

OTHERS

What? What's he saying??

ENRICO

Enough of this. Stop it. I'm sick and tired of all of this.
(Then as if to himself) How dare she come here with her
lover! And so "concerned" about poor crazy me. "Of
course he's crazy or he wouldn't live like this." Did

they ever once even wonder if they were wrong?
Arrogant? Them?? Oh never. The world exists as they
see it—period. I'm not saying we all don't see the world
through our own eyes—you do, but like a bunch of
sheep you wait to be told what you're seeing, and their
kind's happy to tell you, too. And you believe them.
You don't even question them, and god forbid you
were to wake up one day and find yourself labeled,
say "madman" or "mentally ill," forget trying to
convince people that maybe this label is not right,
because as long as people keep repeating it, then the
truth be damned, this becomes the truth!! And I don't
mean just now, it was this way even before I hit my
head falling off the horse.... *(Stops and looks at the
confused men)* "Oh god what is happening?" "Is he
mad?" "Is he not mad?" "Of course he's mad!" In that
case, on your knees! On your knees, I said!

(They fall on their knees.)

ENRICO
Kneel!! Like that. Now touch the ground with your
heads. Three times. One. Two. So you still think I'm
mad. *(Disgusted)* Get up, you goddamn sheep. What
won't you do? Put me in a straitjacket? Crush a man
with the heavy weight of a word? We live our lives
buried under the weight of words, dead words. You
know Enrico IV is long dead, yet you do what he says.
But that's different, you say, this is pretend, out there in
the real world it's different, but is it? Out there the sun
rises new every day. Out there the world awaits. Out
there we do as we wish. Tradition, convention—to hell
with them. We're our own men out there—or are you?!
Are you really free when you mouth the same dead
words, believe the same dead beliefs, live the same
dead lives... *(To BERTHOLD)* You don't understand a
word I'm saying, do you? What's your name?

BERTHOLD
Me? Berthold.

ENRICO

Berthold. What's your real name?

BERTHOLD

Fino.

ENRICO

Fino what?

BERTHOLD

Fino Pagliuca, sire.

ENRICO

(To LANDOLPH*)* And you're Lolo, right? You think I
never heard you talk to each other?

LANDOLPH

Lolo, yes, sire. *(To the others)* Oh my god, he's not mad.

ENRICO

What did you say?

LANDOLPH

I said—

ENRICO

Not mad. Not anymore. No. We've been playing a joke
on those who think I am. *(To* HAROLD*)* Franco, right?

(Turns to ORDULPH.*)*

ORDULPH

Momo.

ENRICO

Momo. Nice name.

LANDOLPH

So he's not—

ENRICO

Funny, isn't it. *(He laughs.)*

OTHERS

He's cured! He's all right!

ENRICO

Sh-sh. Sh-sh. *(To* BERTHOLD*)* You're not laughing.
Something the matter? I wasn't laughing at you.
Some people are called mad just so they can be locked
away. You know why? Because then they can't be
heard. See them? *(Gestures toward the door)* One's a
whore, another's a lech, a third's a quack. No? Don't
believe me—I'm mad! Did you notice how scared they
looked? Who takes what a madman says seriously?
But they let it scare the hell out of them. Why? Why?
Go ahead. Tell me. I'm not going to bite.

BERTHOLD

Maybe they think you're—

ENRICO

I'm going to bite you! I'm going to bite you! I lied!
Berthold!!

BERTHOLD

(Scared) What—??

ENRICO

There. There. You're now as scared as they were—
because you think I'm mad. That's my point.

LANDOLPH

What is?

ENRICO

How unsettling a madman can be. And mad is how
you've thought of me. I unnerve you—or worse—I
shake the ground you stand on. What's it like standing
face to face with a madman as he undermines, rattles
the very foundations of all you believe, all you've
logically thought through and built upon? Madmen,
lucky them, build without rhyme or reason, with all the
direction of the flight of a feather. This way, then that.
One day it's this, one day it's that. For you it's: "Is it
real?" But what is real and what is not? And how do we
know? Because he says it's so? And him and him and a
hundred thousand more? How have these hundred

thousand come to agree what "real" is? Listen to their logic, then ask yourself who's mad. *(Beat)* When I was a child the moon in the puddle was real. Most everything was real then. I liked that. I liked the comfort of that. How important it is then to accept the reality of today, of who we are and who we will become, even if it is so different from who we once were. And how important it is to avoid—as I have not—and here real madness lies—that look through another's eyes—at ourselves, and finding not the person we know we are, but another we think—"can't be me"—a stranger, no more than another beggar on the street, not worth even a look, let alone—a touch... *(Long pause)* It's getting dark.

ORDULPH

The lamp, sire?

ENRICO

"The lamp." Yes! "The lamp!" Don't you think I know that the second I turn my back, head up to bed with my "lamp," you're flicking on the electric lights? In here. In the throne room. I pretend not to notice.

ORDULPH

You want the lights then?

ENRICO

No! You want to blind me? I want my lamp!

ORDULPH

I'll get it.

(Goes out and brings back an ancient lamp)

ENRICO

Ah, some light! Now sit down, around the table, make yourselves comfortable. *(Begins to pose them)* You there. You like—so. I'll sit here. *(He sits.)* A shaft of golden moonlight would be nice right about there. It's good—the moon. We need it. I watch it from my window. Funny how much it must know—that it's not eight hundred years ago and the fellow at the window

is not Enrico IV but just some ordinary man. Look at us!
Look. What a lovely night scene we have here: the
emperor surrounded by his knights! Nice, isn't it?

LANDOLPH
(*Quietly so as not to break the "spell" of the scene*) So it was
all just an act?

ENRICO
What was?

LANDOLPH
Nothing... I mean—Just this morning, I was saying to
him (BERTHOLD)—it's his first day—that given all the
great costumes, and with a room like that one there
(*Throne room*)—We could...

ENRICO
You could what?

LANDOLPH
If we'd known...

ENRICO
That I was—pretending...

LANDOLPH
Which we didn't—

HAROLD
—know. So...

ENRICO
You could have enjoyed yourself more? Had more fun?
Played along?

LANDOLPH
Yes, that's—

ENRICO
Then why didn't you, you idiots? Do you have to have
me, can you do anything on your own? You've had
everything you could possibly need here to lose
yourself in another time. The court of Enrico IV.
Ordulph—the castle of Goslar! You could have gotten

up every morning, dressed up in this fantasy and then
just lived it, breathed it, drunk its air, until it felt more
alive than any other world. Yet it is unreal, you know
this. But how seductive is that? To be able to escape
the real world of the twentieth century where anxiety
reigns, and the heavy burden, the weighted worry upon
every man is: What's going to happen next?

LANDOLPH

I see. I do.

ENRICO

Here, everything's worked out. We know what's going
to happen because it already has.

ORDULPH

Yes.

ENRICO

And sad though may be my fate, awful things
happened to Enrico IV, terrible battles and terrible
times—I know what's coming. And nothing can
change. It's all set. So all that's left is to sit back and
enjoy—act following act, never changing, in exactly the
same way as you knew it would. This comfort has been
yours for the taking. This comfort—of history.

LANDOLPH

Yes. I understand. That's beautiful.

ENRICO

Beautiful, but now gone. Now that you know, it's over.
You had your chance. (*Takes the lamp and is about to
leave*) And I'm tired of it too. (*Almost to himself*) Christ,
she'll be sorry she came here. And dressed up as my
mother-in-law! And him—a monk! Drag along a
doctor? God knows, they may hope to cure me. Clowns.
They'll pay.

(*Knock on the door*)

ENRICO

Who is it?

JOHN

(Off) Deo Gratias.

HAROLD

It's old John, who comes here every night to play the monk.

ORDULPH

Don't tell him anything! Sh-sh.

ENRICO

Why? So you can play a joke on an old man who comes here out of kindness?

LANDOLPH

Don't let on.

ENRICO

I want no one laughing at him. *(Opens the door)* Come in, come in, Father.

(JOHN comes in dressed as a monk.)

ENRICO

My enemies have burned every document favorable to me and my reign. Only one has escaped the destruction, this, my life, written by a humble monk who is devoted to me. And you want to laugh at him! *(Turns to monk)* Sit down, father. Please. Let me move the lamp closer. Write. Write.

JOHN

Whenever you're ready, Majesty.

ENRICO

(Dictating) "The declaration of peace proclaimed at Mayence helped the poor and good, while angering the rich and the bad. It brought food and services to the former, anger and resentment from the latter..."

END OF ACT TWO

ACT THREE

(The "throne room." Dark. In place of the two paintings now stand FRIDA dressed as the Marchioness of Tuscany and DI NOLLI as Enrico IV. They are in the exact positions as were the figures in the paintings.)

(Pause. Door opens, ENRICO enters, holding his lamp. He speaks over his shoulder to the young men and JOHN, whom he is leaving in the adjoining room:)

ENRICO

Don't bother. I can manage. Goodnight. *(He closes the door. Tired and sad, he crosses the room and heads to the door to his apartment.)*

FRIDA

Enrico...

ENRICO

Who is it? *(He suddenly turns.)*

FRIDA

Enrico?

(ENRICO cries out in a panic and drops the lamp. FRIDA, frightened, jumps off the pedestal, screaming:)

FRIDA

Enrico! Enrico! Help!! Help!!

(DI NOLLI jumps down and holds FRIDA, trying to calm her.)

DI NOLLI

I'm here. It's all right. Frida. It's me. It's me.

(MATILDA, *also dressed as "Matilda of Tuscany,"*
BELCREDI, *the* DOCTOR, LANDOLPH, BERTHOLD,
and JOHN *burst in.*)

DOCTOR

Stop! Stop! It's over!

MATILDA

He's cured, Frida! Look at him, he's cured!

DI NOLLI

Cured?

BELCREDI

He's been putting us on. Calm down.

FRIDA

I'm scared. I'm really scared.

MATILDA

There's no reason to be scared. He's not mad.
He's never been mad.

DI NOLLI

That's not true. What are you talking about?

DOCTOR

So it seems.

BELCREDI

That's what they've (*The young men*) been just telling us.

MATILDA

For years he's been pretending. He told them
everything.

DI NOLLI

I don't understand. A few hours ago—

BELCREDI

He was acting. He's been tricking you. And now us,
who only wanted to help.

DI NOLLI

I don't believe it. And his sister, even when she was
dying?

(ENRICO *has stayed at a distance, staring at them.*)

ENRICO

Go on! Tell them.

DI NOLLI

Tell them what?

ENRICO

That it's not just your sister who's dead.

DI NOLLI

My sister? She was your sister who you got to dress up like your mother, Agnes. It was the only way you'd talk to her!

ENRICO

Wasn't she your mother?

DI NOLLI

Of course she was my mother.

ENRICO

Then both sister and mother are dead and gone. You've been stuck up on the wall there (*Gestures toward the pedestal*) so how do you know that I haven't wept myself dry in private over her, even dressed like this.

MATILDA

What's he saying? Sh-sh! Sh-sh!

ENRICO

What am I saying? This: Wasn't Agnes the mother of Enrico IV? (*To* FRIDA *as if to the marchioness*) You, Marchioness, should be able to answer that.

FRIDA

I don't know! I don't know anything!

DOCTOR

The— (*Points to his head*) —is returning. Sh-sh. Everyone!

BELCREDI

I say bull. He's trying to trick us again.

ENRICO

Me? You replace those paintings. He dresses up as
Enrico IV.

BELCREDI

We've had enough of your jokes.

ENRICO

You think this is all a joke?

DOCTOR

Don't get him excited for Christ's sake.

BELCREDI

That's what they (*Young men*) said.

ENRICO

(*To young men*) You? You said all this was a joke?

LANDOLPH

No. Really. All we said was that you were cured.

BELCREDI

I've had enough of this. The "fun's" over; please get
out of those ridiculous costumes.

MATILDA

You shut up. Who cares how anyone's dressed—
if he's cured.

ENRICO

Cured. Yes. I am cured. (*To* BELCREDI) But why leave it
there? Do you know that no one for twenty years has
dared appear before me in clothes like that?

BELCREDI

Sure I knew. Why'd you think I dressed up like a stupid
monk this morning?

ENRICO

Like a monk, yes.

BELCREDI

(*Greeting*) "Peter Damiani!" (*Laughs*) It's funny, but
then—

ENRICO

You thought I was mad. Now that I'm not—it's funny,
isn't it? Everything's funny now. Is she? Dressed like
that? (Points to FRIDA) Jesus, what could you have been
thinking?! (To DOCTOR) You're a doctor, aren't you?

DOCTOR

Yes.

ENRICO

And you were in on all this—dressing her as the
marchioness of Tuscany??! To make fun of me?

MATILDA

No. No! To help you.

DOCTOR

We were trying, not knowing—

ENRICO

Maybe not you. But him (Gestures to BELCREDI) who
thinks everything's a joke.

BELCREDI

You said yourself you're cured.

ENRICO

I'm talking! (To DOCTOR) Do you have any idea, what
you could have done? You could have driven me mad
again. Christ—talking pictures, that jump out of their
frames—

DOCTOR

You saw how we ran in as soon as—

ENRICO

Oh yes! (Looks to FRIDA and DI NOLLI, then at MATILDA,
and finally at his own costume) Look at us. The four of us.
Then and now. What a sight. You're quite the
"magician," Doctor. (Nods to BELCREDI) But all he's
thinking is—when the hell is this masquerade going to
end? (To BELCREDI) Well, now I'll take these (Clothes)
off and come with you. All right?

BELCREDI

With me? Or with us?

ENRICO

Where should we go? The club? In jackets and ties?
Or together to—her (MATILDA's) house?

BELCREDI

Wherever you want. Why would you want to stay
here—the joke's over. I just find it incredible you kept
it up this long.

ENRICO

Ah! You see when my horse fell and I hit my head, I
did, in fact, go mad. Then time passed and I got better.

DOCTOR

But it was a long time?

ENRICO

Yes, Doctor. A very long time. I think maybe twelve
years. (To BELCREDI) And so I lived in complete
ignorance of the world—from that day on. Ignorance
of your life, my friend, your "successes." Life's—
"changes." Of the deceptions of friends, how
everything I'd sought—say a woman's heart—had been
taken by another. Ignorant of everything. I didn't know
who lived or who died. For me such a life wasn't a joke.

BELCREDI

I didn't mean—I meant after—

ENRICO

After? One day— (Turns to DOCTOR) —an interesting
case, Doctor. Take notes. (Continues) Without warning,
one day, the trouble (Points to his head) stopped. Slowly,
very slowly I open my eyes and at first I'm not sure if
I'm awake or asleep. I decide I'm awake. I touch this,
that. The world makes sense again. (Beat) So—he's
(BELCREDI) right, let's end this charade, this nightmare.
Open the windows, I need to breathe life again. Let's
get out of here. (Pulling himself up) But go where? Out

there and be laughed at, pointed out, and whispered
about? "There goes Enrico IV"?

BELCREDI

What are you saying?

MATILDA

You had an accident. You're cured.

ENRICO

They thought I was mad before the accident. (*To*
BELCREDI) You were the worst. You hurt the most.

BELCREDI

I don't remember. If I did, I meant it as a joke.

ENRICO

My hair is grey!

BELCREDI

So is mine!

ENRICO

Mine went grey here, as Enrico IV. There is a difference.
It happened without my knowing. One morning I open
my eyes and suddenly see myself as I really am. How
frightening. I was grey on the outside, and on the inside
as well. The old body was in ruin. I was like the eager
hungry wolf who gets to the banquet only to find it's
over, and cleared away.

BELCREDI

You were not left alone—

ENRICO

True. So many people wanted to help me. Even that
someone who pricked my horse and made him buck.

DI NOLLI

What? What?

ENRICO

Who made him rear back and throw me.

MATILDA

I know nothing about this.

ENRICO

No doubt another joke.

MATILDA

Who did this? Who was behind you?

ENRICO

Who cares now? To all of those at the banquet who left
a scrap for me, Marchioness, or some crumb of pity
or morsel of regret, I thank you. (To DOCTOR) Then it
occurred to me: Why not stay mad? A first, no doubt,
Doctor, in the annals of madness. So quite consciously I
made up this fantasy. And everyone couldn't have been
more helpful. God knows what I was really doing—
trying to make that rock sorry for hitting my head?
Who knows? I began to fill the world—a world that
seemed so empty that day when I opened my eyes—
with our masquerade. Its colors, its beauty, when you
(MATILDA), or rather you (FRIDA)—were its greatest
beauty. So I made everyone pretend with me that we
were back in a moment, which for you was only a
party, but for me—it would become all that was real.
A reality as mad as any madman's. Soon it just grew—
into a throne room, knights, spies, stories played out
day after day. After day. (Turns to the young men)
Why did you tell them I was cured? It doesn't make
sense, if I'm cured, you lose your jobs. Don't you care
about yourselves? That's—madness. Now I'll tell on
you. (To others) They thought we should keep the whole
thing going, after they knew!

BELCREDI

Really. Incredible...

DI NOLLI

(To the young men) You?

ENRICO

Forgive them. It's the clothes. It does things to one. *(He
starts to pluck at his clothes.)* What we wear—we become.
(To BELCREDI*)* Right? Or so it seems, whether we're
aware of it or not. They *(Young men)* are not aware of
it—yet. *(To* BELCREDI*)* But as you know, soon it's second
nature. Dressed like this, here, it's not hard to play
a tragic character. *(Takes a "tragic" pose)* Doctor, I
remember seeing a priest, I think Irish, nice looking,
napping in the November sun, his arm listlessly
dangling along the back of a park bench. Warmed by
the mild afternoon air, which for an Irishman must
have felt almost summery. He sat back, eyes closed,
forgetting who he was, where he was, even that he was
a priest. When a young boy hurried by and happened
to brush his arm, I saw him open his eyes, they were
laughing, his mouth smiling, still dreaming, he knew—
nothing. Then suddenly he remembers, pulls himself
together, straightens his clothes and a seriousness
invades his eyes, much like what you've seen in mine.
The Irish are as serious about Catholicism as I have
been about my kingdom. *(Beat)* I'm cured. So I've had
to act mad, but at least I have done it in private. I pity
you who have to do it in public.

BELCREDI

So everyone's mad.

ENRICO

If you weren't would you be here?

BELCREDI

I came because I thought you were.

ENRICO

And her?

BELCREDI

I don't know. But you've certainly got her attention
with all this: she likes games. *(To* MATILDA*)* Why not
stay here, you've already got the costume.

MATILDA

Shut up.

ENRICO

What I think he's saying is, Marchioness, that history
could repeat itself—as the marchioness of Tuscany,
who could not be my friend, until—Canossa, where
she took me in and pitied me.

BELCREDI

She'll do more than pity you.

ENRICO

What about—"comfort" me?

BELCREDI

She'll do that too.

MATILDA

Stop it!!

ENRICO

Ignore him. I've stopped listening. (To BELCREDI)
You think I give a damn about you? About your life
with her? This is my life. A totally different thing.
You live yours, I'll live mine. (To MATILDA) History
could repeat itself. Is this why you're here? Why you've
come? Why you've dressed yourself like that? Thank
you, Doctor. "As we were. As we are now." But the
mistake you made is that—I know who I am. And he
(DI NOLLI) is not me. Twenty years ago, maybe, not
today. And you (MATILDA), I do not recognize you,
you're completely changed. I don't know who you are.
Her (FRIDA)—I remember. And her I want!!!!! (Moves to
FRIDA) Don't be scared. What a trick they played on
you too, little girl—they got it all wrong. Look at you.
It's a miracle. You are. You live. In the flesh. I want you.
(He grabs her.) I want you!! I want you!! (To the others)
Keep them back! Stay back! I'm ordering you!

(The young men hold the others back.)

BELCREDI

Let go of her. Leave her alone. You're not mad!

(He pushes away the others and approaches ENRICO, *who draws* LANDOLPH'S *sword.)*

ENRICO

I'm not mad, am I?

(He stabs BELCREDI. BELCREDI *screams as others go to help him.)*

DI NOLLI

He stabbed him.

BELCREDI

I'm bleeding.

DOCTOR

I knew this would happen.

FRIDA

Oh god! Oh god!

DI NOLLI

Frida, come here!

MATILDA

He's crazy! He's crazy!

DI NOLLI

Pick him up!

(They start to carry BELCREDI *off.)*

BELCREDI

He's not crazy! He's as sane as I am! He's not crazy!

(They carry him off. Silence. ENRICO *stands looking at the young men who are terrified by what they've just seen.)*

ENRICO

So...I guess it's just us then...together forever.

END OF PLAY